D0833940

IMPRESSIONIST INTERIORS

IMPRESSIONIST INTERIORS

IAIN ZACZEK

STUDIO EDITIONS
LONDON

This edition published 1993 by
Studio Editions Ltd
Princess House, 50 Eastcastle Street
London, W1N 7AP, England

Designed by Michael R Carter
Printed and bound in Singapore

ISBN 1 85891 014 5

INTRODUCTION

Mention the word 'Impressionism' to most people and they will probably think of a landscape. In the public eye, the very essence of the movement was its emphasis on painting in the open air, capturing the ever-changing atmospheric effects that were to be found in Nature. In fact, though, the Impressionists applied their theories to a broad range of subjects, enlivening each of these with the freshness of their approach.

Where interiors were concerned, their chief aim was to employ an unfettered form of naturalism in portraying scenes from modern life. This was more radical than it may sound. The depiction of domestic subjects had a long pedigree in European art but, more often than not, these themes were merely a pretext for illustrating a moral allegory or some sentimental anecdote. Alternatively, they might be valued for their picturesque qualities, as were the many peasant pictures designed specifically for middle-class clients by middle-class painters.

The Impressionists steered well clear of these precedents; regarding themselves neither as social commentators nor as storytellers, but solely as observers. As such, they confined their attention to their own world and concentrated on the purely visual aspects of their subjects. These priorities are perfectly evident in a canvas like Degas' *Women Ironing* (*see* Plate 16). This picture tells us nothing about the women concerned and very little about the process of laundering. Instead, the artist's eye has clearly been attracted by the unusual pose of the stretching and yawning figure.

Degas' decision to focus on such an inelegant gesture was symptomatic of the Impressionists' preference for candour and intimacy in their interiors. Often, this taste manifested itself in an unflattering choice of subject matter. Hence, Degas' bizarre depiction of a relative having a pedicure and Bazille's plaintive portrait of Monet, convalescing in bed after

Women Ironing (detail), *c.* 1884, Degas.
Degas captured the immediacy of the moment with this inelegant but natural pose.

injuring his leg. These were essentially private moments, the sort of occasions when many people might not wish to be seen by their friends, let alone have the episode recorded for public consumption.

The intimacy of such scenes was further highlighted by a subtle, 'fly on the wall' technique, adopted by several of the Impressionists. Many of the figures in their paintings give the appearance of being caught off-guard by the artist. They are shown from behind or frozen in the middle of some reflex action, such as bending, stretching or scratching. Sometimes, this practice was even extended to portraiture where, by definition, the model was expected to be the centre of attention. Thus, for example, in Monet's full-length study of Madame Gaudibert (*see* Plate 4), the subject turns her face away, seemingly unaware of the artist's presence.

This sort of approach frequently lent Impressionist interiors a charming informality, although the results were not always appreciated by the critics. A common complaint was that these paintings were intrusive and bordered on voyeurism. Degas' scenes of women bathing (*see* Plate 17) came in for particular criticism in this regard.

The quest for naturalism received further impetus from the revolutionary advances that were being made in the field of photography.

Madame Gaudibert (detail), 1868, Monet.
Monet gave his model an air of distraction by averting her gaze from the spectator.

Daguerrotypes had been generally available since the 1840s, but it was only when George Eastman simplified the process some 40 years later that photography truly entered the public domain. In 1888, he made the cumbersome paraphernalia of tripods and photographic plates redundant when he introduced the first roll-film camera, marketing it under the enticing slogan: 'You press the button, we do the rest'.

The development of this 'snapshot' form of photography had a huge impact on Impressionism. It enabled artists to go far beyond the limited repertoire of poses that were taught in art schools. Some of these restrictions had been imposed for aesthetic reasons, but many of the novel poses were genuinely too awkward for a model to hold comfortably for any length of time. Also, the Impressionist painters realized that their images did not have to be fully self-contained, but could also represent fragments of a larger reality.

These innovations were reinforced by the growing popularity of Japanese prints in France. On a superficial level, this influence was reflected in the number of oriental accessories that are to be found in paintings of the period, but the Impressionists were also aware of the stylistic implications of these prints. Cassatt and Degas, in particular, were swift to appreciate their use of strong colours and sinuous lines, their repudiation of Western ideas of perspective, and emphasis on decoration.

In responding to these factors, the Impressionists produced a rich variety of interior scenes, echoing the vitality and the immediacy which they had achieved in their landscapes.

—— THE ——
PLATES

PLATE 1
Edgar Degas
The Bellelli Family, 1858 – 60

Degas made many sketches of his Aunt Laura and her family during a stay in Florence in 1858-9, assembling these into a group portrait when he returned to Paris. Some evidence of this composite approach can be found in the contrast between the stiff poses of the figures on the left and the casual gestures of Baron Bellelli and his second daughter.

Laura is shown in mourning for the death of her father, whose portrait hangs behind her. However, her glacial expression also reflects the unhappiness of her marriage. Degas made no attempt to disguise these family tensions and, perhaps for this reason, he never tried to sell the painting. Instead, it remained rolled up in his studio until after his death.

PLATE 2

Edouard Manet

Luncheon in the Studio, 1868

The public reaction to this superbly naturalistic scene highlights many of the problems encountered by the Impressionists. Critics admired the quality of the portraits and the still-life elements but were puzzled by the picture's sense of detachment. What, they wondered, was the precise relationship between these figures? Were such details as the oysters and the armour meant to convey some allegorical message? By refusing to resolve these ambiguities, Manet forced the viewer to concentrate solely on the visual aspects of the painting.

The boy in the boater is Léon Leenhoff. Manet had conducted a twelve year liaison with the youth's mother and was probably his father, although this was kept secret from his family. Manet and Suzanne Leenhoff eventually married in 1863.

PLATE 3

Edouard Manet

Portrait of Emile Zola, 1868

The novelist and critic Emile Zola was a fervent supporter of the Impressionists, recognizing in their works a visual parallel to the naturalism of his own writings. In 1867, he produced a pamphlet containing a highly flattering appraisal of the artist and this portrait was Manet's way of showing his appreciation.

Zola's pamphlet is prominently displayed on the desk, its title also serving as the artist's signature. The background details provide further references to Manet's career. The print by Utamaro and the screen are tokens of his debt to Japanese art, while the reproduction of Velázquez's *The Drinkers* confirms his fondness for Spanish painting. Manet has also included a copy of his *Olympia*, the nude study which caused a scandal at the *Salon* of 1865.

PLATE 4
Claude Monet
Madame Gaudibert, 1868

Monet was in desperate financial straits when he executed this sumptuous portrait. His family, outraged by his affair with Camille Doncieux, had refused to support him; creditors at Le Havre had seized his paintings and auctioned them off; and he had been thrown out of his lodgings at Fécamp. Salvation came in the form of Louis-Joachim Gaudibert, a wealthy businessman and amateur painter. He had bought several seascapes at the auction in Le Havre and provided the artist with an allowance during 1868–9. In return, Monet painted portraits of the patron and his wife. Not surprisingly, the results were comparatively conventional, although the care taken in depicting the sheen of Madame Gaudibert's satin dress and the shine of her varnished table indicate that his interest in capturing the play of light on material surfaces had not abated.

PLATE 5
Claude Monet
The Luncheon, 1868

Monet was staying near Fécamp when this picture was painted, shortly after his patrons, the Gaudiberts, had rescued him from financial ruin. No hint of the artist's money troubles is evident, however, in his charming depiction of his mistress Camille and their young son. Instead, the canvas is notable for the broadly naturalistic manner in which he has lovingly depicted such details as the discarded toys on the floor, the creases in the tablecloth and the fall of light on the cruet set. Monet has also heightened the immediacy of the scene by showing his own place at the table, giving the impression that he has just stepped back for a moment and will soon return to begin his meal.

PLATE 6
Frédéric Bazille
The Artist's Studio, 1870

This relaxed group portrait, set in Bazille's studio in the rue de la Condamine, is a fine illustration of the spirit of solidarity that existed between the Impressionists in the early days of the movement. It is fitting that this particular studio should have been depicted since Bazille, as one of the wealthier members of the circle, often invited his friends to paint there. In the picture, Zola is shown on the stairs, talking with Renoir; the writer and musician Edmond Maître is playing the piano; while, at the easel, Manet explains a point to Monet. The tall figure of Bazille, added later by Manet, is also listening intently to this discussion.

F. Bazille 1870

PLATE 7
Claude Monet
Madame Monet on the Sofa, 1871

Of all the Impressionists, Monet was the most enthusiastic devotee of *plein-air* painting and interiors are comparatively unusual in his work. Nonetheless, this pensive study of his wife illustrates his obvious enjoyment in depicting the play of light on flesh and materials. In addition, the porcelain vase and the fan on the mantelpiece are a reminder of his interest in oriental *objets d'art*. The fan was to reappear in a canvas of 1876, when Monet portrayed his wife in full Japanese costume.

Despite the apparent comfort of her surroundings, Camille Doncieux's relationship with Monet had not been easy. She had been his mistress since 1866 and had been forced to weather the disapproval of his family. The couple married at the end of June 1870, just a few weeks before the outbreak of the Franco-Prussian War, when Monet fled to London to escape military service, leaving his wife behind.

PLATE 8

Edgar Degas
Jeantaud, Linet and Lainé, 1871

During the Franco-Prussian War, Degas served as a lieutenant in the artillery under the command of an old school friend, Henri Rouart. Despite the horror of the occasion, the artist made a number of new acquaintances and three of them are pictured here. The prominent figure in the centre is Pierre Linet, a plaster merchant. Flanking him are two engineers, Charles Jeantaud and Edouard Lainé.

Although this is less ambitious than some of Degas' later portraits, it still shows the artist striving to create an atmosphere of relaxed camaraderie. This is achieved through the careful integration of the three contrasting poses – one figure leans forward intently, the next settles back casually in his chair, and the third reclines on his side. Even so, Degas did not manage to resolve all the compositional problems – note, for example, the awkward posture of Linet's right arm – and the painting remained unfinished.

PLATE 9
Berthe Morisot
The Cradle, 1872

This tender domestic scene was exhibited at the first Impressionist show in 1874. The model was the artist's sister Edma, who had also been a painter until her marriage in 1869. Berthe was particularly adept at handling gentle maternal subjects and this painting is notable for the graceful simplicity of the composition and the delicate rendering of the gauzy drapery around the baby.

Morisot was introduced into the Impressionist circle by Manet and eventually married his younger brother in 1874. She remained a committed member of the group, participating in all but one of their exhibitions.

PLATE 10
Edgar Degas
The Dance Class, *c.*1874

In this justly famous picture, Degas transformed the theme of ballet painting. Instead of depicting one of the principal ballerinas or the glamour of a stage performance, he chose to go behind the scenes to portray a routine rehearsal. The focus of the painting is the ballet-master, Jules Perrot, putting one of the dancers through her paces, but Degas' real interest lay in the relaxed stances of her colleagues. The girl on the piano scratches her back; beside her, a dancer fingers her earring; while, at the far end of the room, ballerinas are adjusting their costumes and stretching. These ungainly actions give the impression that the spectator is looking at an unposed snapshot although, in reality, Degas made detailed preliminary studies for each of the figures.

PLATE 11
Edouard Manet
Lady with Fans, 1873–4

The swirling, fragmented brush-strokes and the languid informality of the pose make this one of Manet's most fully Impressionist works. The sitter was Nina de Callias, the estranged wife of the editor of *Le Figaro*. Born Marie-Anne Gaillard, she was as colourful and exotic a character as the painting suggests. Her salon attracted the cream of Parisian cultural life, including such figures as Mallarmé, Verlaine and Franck. Nina was also a talented poet and composer herself, but her mercurial personality was tainted by a drink problem, leading to her early death at the age of 39.

PLATE 12

Gustave Caillebotte
The Floor Strippers, 1875

This picture caused a sensation when it was shown at the Impressionist exhibition of 1876. Critics were appalled by the vulgarity of the subject and some, worried at the apparent glorification of manual labour, considered it a political statement. In fact, it compares more readily with Degas' washerwomen, as a dispassionate study of human figures involved in a mundane activity. Tradition has it that the scene was painted when the floors in Caillebotte's home were being restored, but experts agree that the job is more usually associated with construction work in new buildings, where humidity has caused the floorboards to buckle.

PLATE 13
Mary Cassatt
Little Girl in a Blue Armchair, 1878

This delightful picture of a young girl sprawling moodily in a huge armchair dates from a critical period in Cassatt's career. Since 1872, she had been gradually establishing a reputation as a *Salon* painter until, in 1877, Degas persuaded her to abandon this respectable course and join the Impressionists. He also assisted her with some of the background details in this painting, one of her first in the new style. However, the risks of attaching herself to such an avant-garde group were soon apparent when the painting was not accepted for the great International Exhibition of 1878. 25 years later, Cassatt could still recall her fury at this decision, particularly when she learned that one of the judges was only a pharmacist.

PLATE 14
Pierre Auguste Renoir
Madame Charpentier and her Children, 1878

The acclaim won by this portrait at the *Salon* of 1879 afforded Renoir his first real taste of official success. Georges Charpentier was an influential publisher and his wife Marguerite was a prominent society hostess. She is pictured here with their children, Georgette and Paul (often mistaken for a girl on account of his dress). Although it appears conventional to modern eyes, the portrait was daring for its time due to the relaxed poses of the sitters and the sketchy background details.

PLATE 15
Edouard Manet
In the Conservatory, 1879

Manet rented the studio of Otto Rosen, a fellow painter, for a nine-month period during 1878–9 and used his conservatory as the setting for this exotic interior. Until recently, conservatories had been the preserve of the very wealthy but, during the Second Empire, the taste spread rapidly to the middle classes and, as if to emphasize this fact, Manet placed a fashionably dressed couple at the heart of the composition. The models were Jules Guillemet and his American wife who, fittingly enough, were the proprietors of a select clothes shop. The painting was not commissioned as a portrait, however, and the detached expressions of the sitters create a mood of ambiguity.

PLATE 16
Edgar Degas
Women Ironing, *c.*1884

Degas once commmented that dancing and laundering were 'two professions... that provide for the modern artist the most picturesque models of women in this time'. Both activities supplied him with a rich repertoire of spontaneous gestures. Here, his eye has been drawn by the contrasting attitudes of physical exertion and fatigue. These poses were his prime concern – an eloquent reminder that Degas was also a sculptor – and the remaining details are only sketchily defined. The wine bottle, incidentally, served a practical purpose: it was used as a mould for pressing shirt-cuffs.

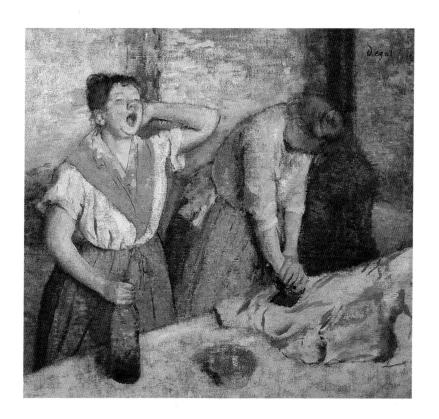

PLATE 17
Edgar Degas
The Tub, 1886

Degas caused a scandal at the final Impressionist show in 1886, when he exhibited a series of pastels of women bathing, drying themselves or having their hair combed. Although no one disputed the technical mastery of these works, many critics baulked at the intimacy of the subject-matter. If the women had been portrayed as goddesses or nymphs, this problem would not have arisen, but Degas deliberately avoided using classical poses for his models, portraying them instead with a candid naturalism.

The dramatic, asymmetrical structure of this composition clearly betrays Degas' fondness for Japanese prints. Note how the slanting line of the shelf bisects the picture and how the artist has used the protruding handle of the brush to link the differing perspectives of the two sections.

PLATE 18
Georges Seurat
Les Poseuses, c.1887–8

Seurat produced two versions of this picture; a large version which is currently in an American collection and this smaller replica. The American canvas was executed in a comparatively naturalistic manner, while the present example was painted in Seurat's characteristic 'pointillist' style. This involved the juxtaposition of small touches of unmixed colour, in order to achieve a vibrant, shimmering effect.

The scene dipicted here is Seurat's cramped studio in the boulevard Clichy. On the back wall we can see part of his most famous work, *Sunday Afternoon on the Island of La Grande Jatte*, the painting which caused a scandal at the final Impressionist exhibition. Critics are divided over the precise theme of the picture. Some maintain that the three figures represent a single woman, shown before, during and after a modelling session. Others believe that this is a portrayal of an audition, during which the artist would choose which model to hire.

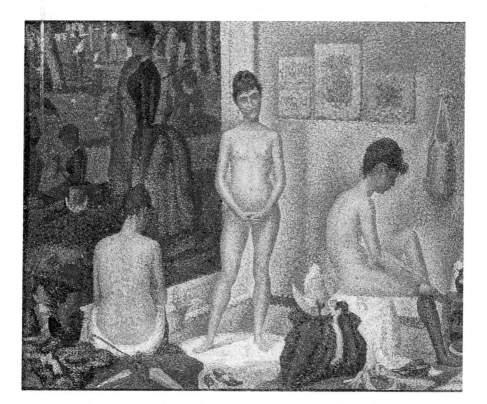

PLATE 19
Vincent van Gogh
Vincent's Bedroom at Arles, 1889

Van Gogh painted this exuberant picture in his 'Yellow House' at Arles, where he was eagerly awaiting the arrival of Gauguin. The bright, flatly painted colours, the strong contours and the lack of shadows all testify to the influence of Japanese prints. Despite the vivid colours, van Gogh saw this as a soothing, restful scene. In a letter to his brother, he explained that 'looking at the picture ought to rest the brain, or rather the imagination'. Some critics have seen the distorted perspective of the room as a sign of the artist's mental instability. In reality, though, this effect was accentuated by the strange dimensions of the room itself, where the far wall was genuinely set at a slanting angle.

PLATE 20
Paul Cézanne
The Card Players, *c.*1890–2

Cézanne painted no fewer than five versions of this subject, a fact which is doubly surprising when one bears in mind his relative lack of interest in portraying human figures. The models were farm labourers at the Jas de Bouffan, his family home near Aix, and the artist has captured perfectly their tense absorption in the game. In doing so, however, he demonstrated just how far he had moved away from his early Impressionist principles. There is nothing transient or accidental in this picture; not a hint of movement. Instead, Cézanne has produced a superbly balanced composition, based around the central axis of the bottle and confirmed by the geometric emphasis on horizontal and vertical lines.

PLATE 21
Pierre Auguste Renoir
Young Girls at the Piano, 1892

Looking at this gentle and harmonious scene, it is hard to imagine that it caused Renoir agonies of indecision. At the start of the year, the Minister of Fine Arts had told the artist that he wished to purchase a new painting for the Musée du Luxembourg. After all the scorn he had endured at the beginning of his career, the idea of a state commission was daunting and Renoir produced no less than six full-size versions of the picture. Interestingly enough, the composition was scarcely altered in these variants and the artist's real concern was over which colour scheme to employ. In the end, he opted for this subtle mixture of russet and pastel shades, which bathe the scene in a mellow, golden glow.

PLATE 22
Paul Cézanne
Woman with a Coffee Pot, 1890 – 4

Cézanne once stated that his aim was to 'make something solid and permanent out of Impressionism, like the art in museums'. This sort of approach is discernible here, where the artist has treated the sitter rather like an element in a still-life composition, giving her the same taut, cylindrical appearance as the coffee pot. The severe expression of the woman, his housekeeper, is understandable, as Cézanne made superhuman demands on the patience of his subjects. When, for example, the dealer Ambroise Vollard asked, after endless sittings, how his portrait was coming along, the painter merely replied that he was 'not dissatisfied with the shirt-front'.

PLATE 23

Mary Cassatt
Mother Combing her Child's Hair, 1898

Cassatt began experimenting with pastels in the 1880s and used them almost exclusively during her visit to the United States in 1898. The sketch-like quality of the medium appealed to her, as to most of the Impression-ists, and it is also responsible for the luminous colouring which she achieved in this scene. By the turn of the century, Cassatt's working relationship with Degas had cooled, although his influence can still be seen in the complexity of some of her designs. However, by concentrating repeatedly on her favourite theme of mothers with children, she gradually lost the immediacy that was central to Impressionism. This picture, for example, comes across as a generalized depiction of maternity rather than as a momentary slice of life.

PLATE 24
Edouard Vuillard
Mother and Child, *c.*1899

Vuillard derived his taste for intimate domestic scenes from the Impressionists and also shared their interest in the decorative possibilities suggested by Japanese prints. Indeed, he developed the latter to such an extent that his figures sometimes appear submerged under the complex patterns of the wallpaper and other materials surrounding them. In addition, his tendency to concentrate on tight, windowless corners of rooms often endows his paintings with a sense of claustrophobia.

The figures here have been tentatively identified as Misia Natanson, the wife of a prominent journalist, and Annette Roussel, Vuillard's niece.

PLATE 25

Vincent van Gogh
Dance Hall at Arles, 1888

This colourful scene depicts the 'Folies Arlésiennes' in the boulevard des Lices, a dance hall that was demolished in the 1920s. It dates from the brief period when van Gogh and Gauguin were working together at Arles. Although they were soon to part company, following their infamous quarrel, there is no mistaking the close artistic bond that existed between them. Here, Vincent's use of pure colours and sinuous contours is strongly reminiscent of Gauguin's experimental Breton paintings. Both men, too, acknowledge an enormous debt to the influence of Japanese printmakers. "Their work is as simple as breathing," Vincent wrote. "They do a figure in a few sure strokes as if it were as simple as buttoning up one's coat.

PICTURE ACKNOWLEDGEMENTS

COVER IMAGE: *Van Gogh's Bedroom at Arles* (detail), 1888, van Gogh − Musée d'Orsay, Paris/Giraudon/ Bridgeman Art Library, London.

FRONTISPIECE: *The Artist's Studio*, 1870, Bazille − Musée d'Orsay, Paris/Bridgeman Art Library, London.

INTRODUCTION: *Women Ironing* (detail), *c*. 1884, Degas − Musée d'Orsay, Paris/Giraudon/Bridgeman Art Library, London. *Madame Gaudibert* (detail), 1868, Monet − Musée d'Orsay, Paris/Giraudon/Bridgeman Art Library, London.

PLATES: 1, 22 (detail) − Louvre, Paris/Bridgeman Art Library, London; 2 − Bayerische Staatsgemaldesammlungen, Munich/Bridgeman Art Libary, London; 3 (detail), 6, 7, 11, 19 − Musée d'Orsay, Paris/Bridgeman Art Library, London; 4 (detail), 8, 9 (detail), 10 (detail), 12, 16 (detail), 17, 20, 23 (detail) − Musée d'Orsay, Paris/Giraudon/Bridgeman Art Library, London, 5 (detail) − Stadelsches Kunstinstitut, Frankfurt/ Bridgeman Art Library, London; 6 − Musée d'Orsay, Paris/Bridgeman Art Library, London; 7 − Musée d'Orsay, Paris/Bridgeman Art Library, London; 13 − National Gallery of Art, Washington. Collection of Mr and Mrs Paul Mellon; 14 − Metropolitan Museum of Art, New York/Bridgeman Art Library, London; 15 − Staatliche Museen Preuss, Kulturbesitz, W Berlin/Bridgeman Art Library, London; 18 − Artemis, Luxembourg/Bridgeman Art Library, London; 21 − Courtauld Institute Galleries, University of London/ Bridgeman Art Library, London; 24 − The Brooklyn Museum, bequest of Mary T Cockcroft; 25 − Glasgow Museums: Art Gallery and Museum, Kelvingrove.